PEARL POETRY PRIZE SERIES

DEBRA MARQUART

FROM SWEETNESS

WINNER OF THE

2000 PEARL POETRY PRIZE

selected by Dorianne Laux

Pearl
Editions

LONG BEACH, CALIFORNIA

Library of Congress Control Number: 2001095533

Copyright © 2002 by Debra Marquart
All Rights Reserved
Printed in the United States of America

Second printing

ISBN 1-888219-19-X

Cover photograph by Jaye R. Phillips

Book design by Marilyn Johnson

PEARL EDITIONS
3030 E. Second Street
Long Beach, California 90803
U.S.A.

In memory of C.W. Truesdale,
editor and friend

Contents

THIS NEW QUIET

FOREWORD

The poems in *From Sweetness* arise from the landscape of rural
North Dakota, from the erotic mind of a woman in love, and
(most powerfully) from the back roads and half-empty club dates of a rock
band scuffling to make it to the next gig. I'm compelled by their various
emotional themes: desire, the brutality of farm life, the ways we are
shaped by family. "On Lake Superior" brings us to the edge of a real and
imaginative shoreline, "an inner ocean," where the narrator asks us to
look at the lake like "a fisherman looks at water/ and sees something
waiting to be caught." Looking again, we see through the eyes of her dead
father, a farmer:

> My father, who is nowhere now, would turn
> and declare Superior and all her rocky shores
>
> an absolute waste. A farmer sees the world
> that way, as so much land in need of planting.

The landscape is also, though more humorously, described through the
eyes of the mother in "The Watkins Man":

> A good thing about living in the country,
> mother says, is you can see trouble coming
>
> from miles away. When the funnel of dust
> rises along the section line, like the white-gloved
> finger of God, we know it's the Watkins man
>
> in his spackled green van full of boar's hair
> brushes and clouded ammonia solutions . . . .

Humor plays an important role in this collection. Poems about the math
teacher Annie K, the ne'er-do-well guitar player Mooch, or the narrator's
"hurricane-like sister" Judy show a deft, almost Dickensian awareness of
character:

What can this woman not make
from the nothing that was given
to her? In the morning, she pops
a Diet Coke, torches a Marlboro,
inhales her usual breakfast.

In the early light, I watch
the curtain blow behind her,
the smoke curling in tendrils
through her hair. In the Bible,

Judith is dangerous, only allowed
in the Apocrypha, and Deborah
is the singer of songs, the leader
of troops into battle. Oh, the plans

our mother had when she named us.

Simple wisdoms arise from these character studies, but the true strength
of this book lies in the poems about rock and roll. Poems like "Wearing
Dead Women's Clothes" (about thrift store shopping on the road), "Our
Common Friend," (about a bass player):

from a local metal band . . . swaying
his tight-crotch hips, and angling,

just so, a reflective mirror pick-guard
he'd installed on his Fender
precision bass so the spotlight

threw a sharp beam . . . into the eyes
of the chosen woman, now blinded . . .

These set pieces have a charming backstage quality about them and are
based on a musician's funky awareness. In "Big Guitar Sound" the band
equipment takes on a life of its own in the same way that the writer revels
in the sway and jangle of language:

> a thick shimmering sound rising,
> the wah, wah, the super fuzz,
>
> the hyperturbo overdrive groove
> phase shifter that made him sound
> like thirteen chain saws gnawing
>
> through walls, a continent away . . .

We also see the band behind the closed doors of hotels where they spend the nights with their grief and uncertainty, their youthful sorrow and resignation. "This New Quiet" begins:

> The day after the fire, all their equipment
> charred in a ditch and blown to ashes
> the thin axle of the truck lying on its side
>
> like the burnt-out frame of a dragonfly,
> they gathered in a circle of old couches,
> most of them sitting forward, their eyes
>
> studying the swirls in the worn carpet.
> They who had the power to make
> so much noise sat in this new quiet.

These are poems of a world rendered specifically, characters lovingly articulated, landscapes redolent with possibility and life. I'm drawn to their honesty and vision and the sounds of their making, a music that's particularly American.

—*Dorianne Laux*
Eugene, Oregon

The open palm of desire wants everything,
wants everything, wants everything.

—Paul Simon, "Further to Fly"

IN A COOL DARK TONGUE

OTHER KNOWLEDGE

Somewhere in this hot city he sleeps,
tangled in rough sheets, his body

twisted in the shape of a question.
If he knocked on this loosely hung door

I would remove the chain and answer
all he asks, my skin scrubbed clean,

smelling of green apples and lemons.
How I want to trace with my hands

the slow curve of his back. Lover,
I would say, lie down on the cool

sheets and let me wash the salt
from your skin. How long have we held

our breath, swimming deep strokes
to meet in these murky waters, how long

have we heard this music, soft and dark
as the inside of a womb. You say

you're from a large southern city,
but I have other knowledge.

I rattled you out of the sand
with my shaker noisemakers,

one egg in each hand, dancing
in circles, chanting the names

we use only in sleep. Did you know
the aborigine man dreams the spirit

of a child, then comes home to love
his wife, saying, Today I saw a child,

and now I have planted it in your womb.
If you knock, the chains will dissolve

in your hands. Inside, find me brewing
a mixture of spearmint and cloves.

Lie back, let me trace this bayleaf,
soft as a feather down the smooth line

of your stomach. In a cool dark tongue,
perhaps it will find words for us to speak,

saying, Love this woman, you've been
adrift in the open sea for too long.

How Bad News Comes

A telephone rings
like an emergency
six times each minute
in a room down
the hall. I think
of the one to whom
bad news is coming.
At the market,
she touches fruit.
Driving home,
she strums her fingers
on the steering wheel.
She hums with the radio
and thinks of her lover,
the one she's left
behind, or the one
she will see again,
remembers the soft heat
of his breath, the urgency
of his belly against hers.
This is the way life
insists on itself, his scent
still on her as she reaches
for the phone. Happy
to catch it in mid-ring,
she comes through
the door, leaves her keys
dangling in the lock.
She leans in, unclips
an earring, to hear
the voice on the other end
saying, *I've got some*
bad news, feeling

in that long moment
before the words come,
the difference between
the way it was
and the way
it will be, that moment
before the groceries
fall to the floor.

ON LAKE SUPERIOR

What returns us to these shores, the promise
of fish, something silver flashing through our veins.

I walk the long pier, past the rollerbladers,
bowlegged in their kneepads, past the children

tossing popcorn to gulls. On the edge
of this great inner ocean, we are all tourists,

a light circling overhead, calling us like sailors,
home. And we are lovers, kissing against the rail,

turning our faces to our collars in the cold
spray of waves. A fisherman looks at water

and sees something waiting to be caught.
My father, who is nowhere now, would turn

and declare Superior and all her rocky shores
an absolute waste. A farmer sees the world

that way, as so much land in need of planting.
I've abandoned despair, that miserable lifeboat.

The water does not care enough to care
nothing for me. From the street, the creak

of a carriage, horses' hooves on cobblestone,
that old, old poetry. The wind blows tones

tonight, a saxophone, on the boardwalk,
breathing in, breathing out, the blue smoke

of a song I know but can't recall. A stone
rides deep in my belly. Soon I must return

to my small river, go down to the shore
and beat my clothes against the hardness,

open my throat and try to make a song
from the long ago row of notes.

BEATING UP THE BROTHER

Because he was a single stalk
of sweet corn in a prairie
of sisters, because we were seven,

nine, eleven, and twelve, and he
was only ten—the middle one,
the fulcrum our farm rested on.

Because he was too cute
and wore short pants, little hand
in the cookie jar, little shrug

and grin. Because his buzz cut
felt like a freshly mowed lawn
when we drove our hands

over it, because Mom and Dad
left us alone on Saturday nights
to watch the Ed Sullivan show and

the Miss America Pageant, because
no beauty from Dakota ever won,
or advanced to the final round

of ten, because we were a gaggle
of girls, expected to fly away,
and he would stay to plow

the land after we were gone.
Because he was the only boy,
sweet-natured and forgiving

as Jesus under our fists, because
he was the brother, had that part
we thought of as extra, that part

we had never seen but knew existed.

My Husband, a City Boy, Decides To Buy a Truck

When I find him, he's lying on the bed
with magazines, surrounded by glossy
spreads, the fleshy airbrushed tones

of break-your-neck-beautiful pickup
trucks, their commercials promising
added leg-room, adventure in ownership,

and deliverance from all life's hard, stuck
places. Rock guitars chime with whiskey
voices about narrow misses, rugged

times survived, all thanks to the solid
dependability of a 4 x 4. This is how
it will be: you arrive in your truck

(AKA, the rock) loaded down with fun-
loving girls wearing tank tops and short,
fringed cut-offs. They hop from the cab

tossing their glossy hair to find the next
available good time. In the back are guitars
and amplifiers, and silver kegs full of

piss-warm beer. Believe me, you'll kiss
yourself then for having the horsepower.
This is the new truck, he says. Gone

are the days of gun racks and roped deer,
tires kicking up tufts of dirt, the dark
shrinking silhouette of a cowboy hat

as the truck climbs the last rise. For me,
it was hay bales, straw bales, alfalfa bales,
rocks, rocks and more rocks, cranky

stick shifts, slippery clutches, feet barely
reaching the pedals, driving lunch out
to Dad in the August fields, dust and sweat-

slicked seats, the smell of oil and tractor
grease, the thunk and tumble of gas cans
rolling in the back. Listen, I tell him,

here are three things I'd like to never
again do: wear a seed cap, live in
a trailer park, and own a pickup truck.

Eventually I add, *wear safety orange*,
to the list, but that's years later
and another story altogether

THE WATKINS MAN

Ever since the Kirby man sold Grandmother
the Electro-Lux No-Fuss by shampooing
to sparkling brilliance a five-inch circle

in the dead walking center of her carpet,
so that she had to buy the magnificent beast
with all its twenty-five purring parts

(the linoleum sweeper, the edge cleaner,
and the motorized attachment that doubles
as a belt sander) to get the rest of the rug

to match, we are not at home to salesmen.
A good thing about living in the country,
mother says, is you can see trouble coming

from miles away. When the funnel of dust
rises along the section line, like the white-gloved
finger of God, we know it's the Watkins man

in his spackled green van full of boar's hair
brushes and clouded ammonia solutions
that bristle and slosh to the road's dips

and curves. Get down, Mother yells.
We suck it up and dive like infantry
at Guadalcanal, our noses pressed

into Mother's waxy hardwood. Outside,
the Watkins man, his nose pickled,
his pores deep as canyons, knocks

his ham-hock fists on our weatherbeaten,
never locked door. We wait, twelve eyes
breathless, staring, for the screen door's

report against the frame, for the slippy slap
of shoes receding. Wait for the car door
slam's ricochet off the barn, the worried

zing of his engine, the neck-craning
turnaround crunch of gravel, before we rise,
dust ourselves, collapse together in laughter

and relief. We know he's just an honest man
trying to make a living, but he shouldn't
have tried to show Mother, that one time,

the fishy handfuls of dust, the sloughed-off
human scales that lurk infectious in our
mattresses. He just shouldn't have done that.

Envy of Origins

Wipe the dust from your face
gravel road girl, your childhood spent,
not on Wordsworth or Keats,

but on the intricate hoisting
of hay bales to a hip.
How you were made

for lifting—books pulled
from your hands, shoulders
pushed outdoors to fresh air.

You walked the gravel roads,
endless miles, eyes cast down,
reading the stones' etched

faces. Lift your eyes now,
move aside for the poetess
who storms through in long skirts,

boasting of days whiled away
with Auden, evenings spent
with Edna St. Vincent Millay,

all the rainy mornings,
and dusty libraries of childhood.
Admire the antique earrings

plucked from a safe back East
(where all the family heirlooms
are kept). With not a piece

of china or a silver engraving
to recommend you, what are your
treasures? The grandmother

who left the world screaming
bloody childbirth, the grandfather
crossing the Volga under cover

of darkness, their bones buried
deep in the vault of earth. How
will you raise them? Think

how you invented games
as a child, playing catch
with yourself, when no one

threw the ball back, recall
the loud whack against
the side of the barn,

the hard thunk of return
in your palm. And no matter
how you complicated things,

spinning tricky English,
throwing odd angles, always
the ball found its point

of origin, always your hips
divined the trajectory,
always your hands knew

where they must be next.

THE FALLING MAN

How I wanted to touch the stitching
of his wrist brace that summer he fell
from his bike. Perched on the stoop
with his backpack, he showed me

the crisscross and I wanted to undo it,
lay my hands on the perfect hairline
fracture. And how I wanted to trace
the faint stitching scar on his shin,

cauterize it with my own heat the next
summer when he also fell from his bike,
the rusty chain breaking free, the toothy
links circling his ankle. And though

I wondered about him always falling
from bikes, I admired him for being man
enough to cry in front of the women,
and for later telling me, a woman

he didn't know wouldn't laugh,
that he had cried. And so I took to
reading his horoscope every morning,
wondering what kind of a day

he was having, and I grew jealous
of the shower water rolling in clear
innocuous rivulets down his body,
and I hated the impervious cotton sheets

that touched him each morning as he rolled over,
that first moment of waking, reaching for himself,
as any man does. And I envied the warm
lucky life of his backpack, and the strings

of his work apron that tied so thoughtlessly
around his waist, and the long, looping straps
of his tank top that conspired to expose
the ripples and flanks of his chest, which

I studied for many long minutes that night
of his twenty-fourth birthday before thrusting
out my stiff arm in congratulations
to avert the hug that was certain to give me

heart failure. And when I pointed to
the slim scar high on his forehead, he said
he had fallen from a great height as a child
and I said, *Oh, now I'm starting to see all*

your faults, which made both of us laugh
out loud. This man, so steady on his feet
around me, those years I waited for him
to waver, to trip, to swagger, to sway.

Those years I waited for him to fall
headlong into my strange wild arms.

MY CATHOLIC TONGUE

She's like a surly bank robber, this new hygienist,
in her face mask and goggles, nervous about
silent alarms and the time this is all taking.

She cracks my mouth like a vault, scans
the perimeter as if for surveillance equipment.
As soon as she's in, she taps the gleaming

gold fillings and runs the scaler across my gums,
her deep pricks looking for redness, soreness,
the telltale signs of the dreaded gingivitis,

so she can call the dentist, drilling and tapping
in the other room, and, in an important voice
say, *Here, take a look at what I found.* My tongue

follows her like an ineffectual security guard
in a crisp uniform and badge, with no gun
or holster. Armed with simple vigilance,

the curious tip is wrestled to the floor,
held by the long arm of her tiny probing mirror.
Hard at work now, the curette chips away.

Ripping plaque, pieces flying free like plaster
off a concealing wall, she asks, in a cool voice,
Do you floss each day? My Catholic tongue,

ever the stoolie, wants to confess, but waggles,
Un-hungh. I fade and lapse under the pressure
of her instruments, the sharp prong of the scaler

returning for clean up, scoping out the crevices,
the dark places where all treasure can be found,
the mirror's bright aluminum head craning side

to side, saying, *Are you a cavity, are you a cavity,
are you,* looking for my dirty den of neglect.
The sympathetic nodding hook of the curette

returning, saying, *See, we could have been friends.*
My tongue lying low, hissing silently to itself
the precise location of the mother lode.

LIGHT SWEET CRUDE

A patriot is not a weapon . . . .
A patriot is a citizen trying to wake
from the burnt-out dream of innocence.
                                    —Adrienne Rich

At midnight in the produce section
I think about the old woman on CNN
who stood on the rubble of her
white stone house and raged
at the camera in a wild Arabic tongue,
the cords of her neck straining. Civilian,

she screamed. *Civilian.* Her only English word.
Inside, children lie crushed in beds
like corsages in Bibles. The camera scans
the wreckage—dishes and cups broken
into fragments, a water gourd once round
and smooth as a baby's head, now smashed

entirely open. Halfway across the world
they're dropping bombs. All night,
from inside the deep land cushion
of the Middle West, I watch this great
fireworks display of war. All day at work
the talk is of how many sorties flown,

how many Xs obliterated, how many people
ran like ants out of the cross hairs
of a missile. As the ten-millionth
screw in the great roaring machinery
of business, my job is not to question
the dropping of bombs. Halfway across

the world, where light sweet crude
bubbles up from the sand, they are
dropping bombs, and tonight
in the produce section, I'm struck
by the violence of even this fruit—
the lengths my country will go

to deliver the juicy acres of peaches,
kiwi and grapes, the seven kinds
of apples in February, all laid out
in polished rows for my inspection.
Halfway across the world
they're dropping bombs

on my behalf. Get that fruit
away from me. I will not eat it.

WITHIN MOMENTS
—Sarajevo, 1994

Some French photographer has captured
this moment—a woman in a gray coat,

fallen face down to the pavement,
moments after the mortar rounds

have stopped. From the triangle
of her scarf, a pool of blood spreads

gray and thick as oil. Her boots
are turned inward, her shoulders

crumpled under like some ruined
and forgotten thing. See how quickly

she has joined the legion of the dead.
Moments ago she was a woman

hurrying to an errand. Now
the boy with a gray bag in his hands

climbing the stairs does not stop
to check her pulse. Even as his eyes

glance back, his right leg veers out
of the photo. And the two men

in uniform coming up from the dark
subway, lift their legs and look at her

with the same mark of exhaustion.
Later, someone will remove her

to the morgue where attendants
will find this message nestled

in her pocket, the reason she is out
today, to deliver this letter

to the Red Cross for a granddaughter
on the other side of the fighting.

Thank God, the note will read,
that you are all alive and well,

and thank God, that we
are all alive and well.

From Sweetness

What was the taste of him beneath
the sprinkles that fell from pastries,
the éclairs and Bismarcks, the jelly

donuts in the box on the table
in the break room behind the Line of Fire
shooting range (don't ask) where we talked

for hours. The sugary blue
half moons and thin yellow stars
that he dabbed with his wet finger

and brought to his mouth time and
(agonizing) time again, the sweetness
dissolving on his tongue as rounds

of ammo popped off. Outside the door,
men in goggles in a lock-legged stance
aimed at silhouettes, intruders

flying toward us on long pulleys,
tattered and riddled with bullet holes
to be examined for accuracy of firing.

And with me so terrified of handguns
and small talk, what held me there
next to his velvet presence, content

to imagine the collection of sprinkles
dissolving on his tongue (all the while
thanking God for my excellent

peripheral vision). And where
was the word (yes) on my tongue
in the parking lot, when he asked

in his no-one-but-you voice
who wanted to go for burgers,
causing me to recall someone

who waited, hungry, at home.
Amazing, how the body recovers,
finds the car keys in the messy bag,

the jagged teeth of the ignition,
grinds for reverse, first, navigates
the long left loop onto the freeway.

When will we know if we've made
a mistake? Impossible to count
the times I've turned back, slipped

my body into the booth, felt
the length of his thigh lining mine,
imagined the thin fries delivered,

crisp and sizzling in their checkered
basket for devouring, watched
their small journey, one by one,

from the dab of ketchup to the tip
of his tongue. Sometimes my own hand
reaches in to touch his wrist, directs

the oily gold from his fingertips
to my lips. So bad for me (I know)
so good. The taste of salt

that follows so much sweetness.

Our Gold and Yellow Making

DRATS

What becomes of them, the cousins
who call late at night, a little drunk
they admit, and wanting to talk about

the crimes of the first lady, their hopes
for her future imprisonment. We are bound
together by this blood, the love our fathers

never spoke. What do teenagers care of curses
before birth, that old-land-brother-hunger?
The earth was dirt to us, and the ripened

wheat singing to mud flaps on his father's pickup
on my father's land was background noise
to back road drives, where we parked to talk

of gradations of blood relation to the radio's
lighted dial. Is it too late to recall that word
we discovered scratched on the chemistry

desk's obsidian surface—*Drats*. Carved,
we theorized, by some dome-headed farmboy
destined to firebomb into the South Pacific

or be sucked through the combine's irresistible
conveyor. And when Mr. Dewald's questions
about the shared properties of matter eluded us,

we would mouth that word, *drats*, a Bunsen
burner flaring between us, and understand
fusion. Revolutions undo us, our blood

divided and divided again. No wonder
we held tight the twining taper. Here
is the empty motel room he calls from

twenty years later, the beer can pop-top
hissing through silence, the spout
of alcohol and politics. Here we are,

cousin, out in the world, just as you
predicted, among strangers who
would never guess our secrets.

What remains for me to confess—
the children I left you to never have?
Our fathers, those brothers, lie together

now in the rise near the field where
we lay. See how things come around?
When you call, if you like, we can work

the dark nubby root between us and gorge
at the table of family hurt. But don't ever
slur and ask me that question again:

Hey, is this where all the cool people live?

My Father's Wallet

Small curve of leather that rode
on his backside in the pickup
to auctions every Tuesday,

that stretched and marked
the right pocket of his Levis,
that padded the wood chairs

of the café where he gossiped
with other farmers about
grain yields, corn futures,

that rests now in the cupboard
above the sewing machine
like an upturned turtle shell

abandoned among spools
of thread, jars of buttons,
where Mother put it after

she cleared away his fifteen
trim suits, his thirty shirts,
his pajamas and robe, his neat

row of shoes. His pickup
sits undriven in the left bay
of the garage. Only the wallet

remains, packed, as he left it,
with plastic cards, photo IDs,
gold membership numbers,

the unspent fifty dollars
and the unused lines of credit
we all hope will someday

save us. At the White Knights
Casino we plug the slots
for him, for the big lotto payoff,

waiting for his always earthly
luck to rub off on us.
But everything comes up lemons,

oranges, diamonds, flags,
and rubies in the wrong
combinations—the mixed bag

of fruits and wild cards
that never fell in place the way
we'd always hoped or expected.

Usual Magic

Remember rooster, that cock
with his deep blue, oil-in-water
feathers? How he envied our gold

and yellow making. Mornings,
he hated the weakest chick.
In the afternoon, he loathed

the strongest. Every night
he tucked his bruised comb under
his pinfeathers and secretly despised

the rest. Even Mary Jane Bitz,
our sister's friend, with her sleek black
ponytail and her midnight blue racer.

He hopped on the metal runner
as she pedaled our gravel drive,
and pecked her on the back,

saying, Get *out, get out, get out*
of my yard. No one makes anything
here without me. It wasn't sad

when Mother had to take him
to the stump. The next day
the sun rose and rose again

without his awful noise,
and the small round wonders
appeared in the straw beds

by their usual magic.

Annie K and
the Function of Y

Under the half moon of her glasses
and the radiator's disapproving hiss,
under the silent footfall behind us,

we crunched numbers, calculated
coefficients. We called her Annie K
behind her hammy back, Mrs. Leier

or nothing to her face. Her wool suits
were iron-chested, World War Two,
double-breasted. Her cinched-in

waist vexed and fretted, the hour
we spent in math each day with her.
On the slippery pyramid of her

formulations, I was failing, failing,
falling down the architectonic steps
of her equations. The unknowns

were like Catholic gods to me,
sequestered in heaven, and speaking
only Latin. She fussed over the brainy

boys, backtracked if they faltered.
Her eyes extrapolated my short list
of variables—my hands would work

the stove, the plow, the milker,
my pen confined to thank you notes,
to-do lists. Never marry a man

in your own profession, she said
one day to the ceiling (the only lesson
I took from calculus). The squish

and wobble of her shoes unnerved us,
those stamped-down, high-heel patrols.
We bent our heads, speculated the value

of y to the worried whisper of erasers.
We scrutinized the inscrutable cosine
to the rustle and swish of her girdle,

factoring the unknowns lurking
beneath her skirts. And the spider web
ganglion of leg hair, trapped and

matted under her support hose,
was final proof to us of what
she thought inconsequential

and of no significance whatsoever.

Thinning the Litter

The fourth daughter out of five children,
the youngest girl, worries her whole life

about the litter of kittens, afraid to take
the last piece of bread after watching

the strong wrestle the milky teat from
the weak. The fourth daughter, afraid

to take the last piece of pizza, the last
kernels of corn, scoop them up in one

clean swipe, stubborn mouth refusing
to eat or speak. The fourth daughter

out of five children on the farm, forced
to thin the litter, to choose the survivors—

the white one, the black one, the star-marked
one—understanding the signs of favor,

the signs of disfavor. The fourth daughter
out of five children on a farm takes

the brown burlap bag, the brick,
takes the knocks on the side of the barn.

THE HARDNESS OF MATH

Grade school dance.
Too much patent leather

and the slither of slips
under cotton dresses.

Cafeteria tables stacked
into corners, and streamers

twisting from rafters.
In the air, the mix

of floor wax and peanut butter,
as a boy and a girl dance toe

to toe, talking about the hardness
of math. The record player

spinning 45s as the boy
and girl dance hip bone

to hip bone, the small
beginning of something

rising between them.

OLDER SISTER

Forever, she rides
in front of me
on the school bus,
a lime-green mohair
draped over pale
shoulders, her stiff
auburn flip bouncing
firmly. In the curved
mirror of the mahogany
dressing table, she teases,
rats, and sprays her hair
into submission. Year
after year, her class photos
reflect magazine-rack
knowledge of the properly
curving eyebrow,
the correct application
of blush to the cheek.
No sweaty back seats
on her conscience,
no cigarettes in her
drawers. The older sister
wore bras that fit
and skirts that covered
the knee. The older sister
never used one more
chocolate chip
than the recipe required.

Hurricane

When hurricane rolls into town,
her wide-bottomed Ford blowing
blue plumes of diesel, her muffler
scraping sparks, the barometer rises

twelve degrees. The weatherman
develops a twitch in his neck.
When Judy hits town, her billfold
wadded with cash, headed for

the wide-open space of the mall,
she leaves her Ford parked at a crazy
angle across the yellow grid.
At the peanut bar, over the foam

of a Big Top beer she yanks
an accordion of photos from
her purse, the five children
she raised *without that asshole*—

perfect teeth, perfect skin, perfect
ACTs, the youngest, a single cell
split perfectly from her body.
What can this woman not make

from the nothing that was given
to her? In the morning, she pops
a Diet Coke, torches a Marlboro,
inhales her usual breakfast.

In the early light, I watch
the curtain blow behind her,
the smoke curling in tendrils
through her hair. In the Bible,

Judith is dangerous, only allowed
in the Apocrypha, and Deborah
is the singer of songs, the leader
of troops into battle. Oh, the plans

our mother had when she named us.
In school, they called her *twee-twunk*,
because of her thunder thighs,
and her unpronounceable *R*s.

This morning, I want to call her
by her rightful name—bear woman,
force of nature, sister. This morning,
I want to call her sister.

FROM THE DESK OF THEM

The gals share a private joke with the world
and their tired husbands. They go on long trips

alone, or with other gals. Taking their lunch
downtown, they plan church cookbooks,

tell the waiter dirty jokes, laugh and pretend
to blush. Throwing their diamond-ringed

fingers up in public, they fan their faces
with their napkins and say, *Is it hot in here*

or is it me? They enjoy sex, we know,
and are responsible for sending out all

high school reunion letters. Later in life,
they move into interior design, wear chic

crepe dresses, have maids and secretaries,
and stationery, which is from the desk of them.

HEARING
MY MOTHER'S VOICE

The blinking telephone reminds me
to unwind the tape, let loose

the voices that have called me.
I unbutton my blouse, pull on

a sweatshirt. Time to let go
of the meetings, the commute,

what my boss said in passing.
I recognize her voice even from

the other room, anxious breath
on the line, the ends of words

clamped tight. Her voice rises
at the end of each sentence,

as if forever asking. The one time
she visited, she quizzed me again

and again, *Now, to get back on
the freeway, do I go right and follow*

*the loop, or go under the highway
and turn left?* In her small town

there's not even a yellow light
flashing caution. Beside the phone

now I rewind the tape, listen again
for the details, the heavy breath,

the vowels that refuse to sing. I find
it's me, calling home earlier in the day

telling whoever gets this message
to pick up some bread, some milk,

and asking, in a small voice,
what we will be doing tonight?

AFTER WE MAKE LOVE,
THE PHONE RINGS

He pulls the receiver
across the white sheets.
I study the hollows
of his cheeks, so deep
in the half light.

The silence becomes
the voice of his mother
returning his call.
What does he want?
she asks. Her words

a small buzzing in
his ear. Nothing,
he says, falling back,
a solid thump
on the sheets,

the dark cord
glistening in a curl
up his abdomen.
Just thought
I'd let you know,

he twirls the cord
on his finger,
that I won't
be home for dinner.
And they laugh

that easy laugh
between them.
It's funny because
he's a moved-away son,
and hasn't eaten

at home for years.

MORE LIKE HUNGER

Oh peach, let me rest for a time
beneath the sway of your branches.

Tell me again about the fever
of your childhood, the gold teeth

of your youth. Then shall we
join hands and recount the many

differences between us. I've come,
exhausted, from a world marked

by your arrivals, full of rooms
made too large and luminous

by your absence. In the great
maw of days, I struggle to recall

the rumble of your voice moving
through empty rooms like thunder,

no, more like hunger. Once I believed
the world would drop with succulence,

always in my lap. So long ago fallen,
I lie in this bed, heavy with sweetness,

imagining the swell and curve
of you. Listen, inside each of us

is a hard pit that wants to be stripped
free. And underneath, a grainy hollow

with deep grooves and wild unbroken
threads, never before seen,

and longing to be licked clean.

ALCHEMY

Just because all of our computers
aren't put in a row doesn't mean they're
not an assembly line.
                              —Nancy Reinecke

It's hard, this business
of turning straw into gold.
Every day someone's coming

to your door, saying, Gimme,
gimme, gimme what you got,
and you turn over these soft

round kernels, spun fresh
from the smooth yolk
of your body. They slip

them deep in their pockets,
calculating the value
per gram, what the market

will allow. People agree
that nothing is ever lost,
only changed to other forms.

This glowing humming
inside you, the reason
you're confined to mining

the day's details down
to something pulsing
and new. It's a mystery

why you stay. See, others
are running in the moonlight,
shouting, Lovers, bring me more

lovers. You watch them from
the balcony, your breath
rising and falling, throwing words,

throwing curses to the vacancies,
your hands moving in strange,
unaccountable ways. Busy again,

at making something out of
what other people thought
was nothing.

FISH WHILE YOU CAN

—for Mark Vinz

Let's not end up like our man,
Alfie, in the nursing home
messing his pants and raving
about metal lures and tangled lines.
As the nurses turn him to change
his soiled sheets, he's pulling in
the big one. Careful, he yells
at the attendant, his arms caught
in casting pose. *Hold on to him
now. Hold on.* Dark is the body
of water below him, the lake turns
to river turns to sea. Each year
we write letters to each other
about the poems we know
will get away until next summer
or better weather. I want
a moment each day like the one
I saw in a movie—two kids sitting
in a rowboat in the middle
of an enchanted lake
as rainbow-skinned trout leap
in wide arcs into their arms.
Why do we settle, each year,
for tin cans and bottom feeders,
for poems like old boots,
their drunk tongues refusing
to speak. Listen, something
waits for us. The lake turns
to river turns to sea. Careful now,
easy with the line. *Easy.*
Ah man, she's a beauty.

May All Our Children Swim

—Family Reunion, Holiday Inn

Could it be the grandparents who watch us?
The unbroken line of six Josephs, the Marys
and Barbaras who spread their bones from

the steppes to the plains, rising in a silent
column behind us. They who were broken
as they broke the land so that we might

vacation in this state of ten thousand lakes.
In turn, we hover in the balcony
like squatters, overlooking our children

who swim in the kidney-shaped pool.
Feeling one generation away from
poolside, we sit in vacation clothes,

crisp from their packages. We shuffle
our creamy white feet in unfamiliar
sandals and throw caution like life

preservers over the railing—*Don't forget
your earplugs. Stay out of the deep end.*
Born too soon for city pools, destined

to work hardscrabble, we worry about
our swimming children. If one of them
goes down, who among us could save

a drowning child? Below, the true citizens,
barefoot and swaddled in fluffy robes,
lounge and drink poolside. Snapping

their fingers for waiters in bow ties
who bend to deliver trays of appetizers,
cold beers, room tabs to sign. The class

of sixty-five is here, the marquee
announces—a thirty-year reunion.
The two girls voted best personality

and class clown, dressed in draping black,
stand on the edge of the deep end.
They shed their big gold shoes, plug

their noses, hold hands and plunge
in a large splashing roll. They surface
with a giant roar that explodes

to the rafters, reaching us in the balcony,
our faces drawn with worry as we watch
our youngest, small and pink—our little

peanut floating along with the big kids,
a green rubber turtle ringing her waist.
Confident of her equipment, she holds

her nose, throws her body back and kicks
in a wild dog paddle. She works at this
for hours, her tongue bent with

determination, as we watch amazed
at how easily she rises, her body breaking
the plane again and again. Who knows

what the grandparents make of this?
Imagine—our young, floating along,
so buoyant on the untroubled surface.

THIS NEW QUIET

WEARING DEAD
WOMEN'S CLOTHES

Remember the Mormon thrift store
in Idaho, as big and tidy as a Kmart,
where Wanda rifled through the racks

and found me a sealskin coat
that was practically new and warm
as the French Riviera. We'd run

headlong into the cold wild west
with nothing but our little black
dresses, good for shaking tail

and singing doo-wop. I was colder
than Canada. How I wanted
that dark fur around me, but I worried

about the baby seals. I'd seen it on TV—
bearded men with clubs waiting
on beaches in places as remote

as Newfoundland. Wearing fur,
I said, creates a market. Honey,
she said, her voice rising an octave,

her curved fingernails, long and sharp
as harpoons, that's the advantage
of wearing dead women's clothes.

They take all that bad karma
with them when they go. I still have
the sweatshirt she gave me in Ames

when I was sick and all the clothes
in my suitcase were spandex
and leather and sweated clean through.

In the motel room, she peeled
the layers from me and swabbed
my body cool with a cloth. I lay

panting on the damp sheets
like something stripped clean
and brand new. Wanda,

I blubbered before the pills
knocked me out, my problem
is that I wasn't properly mothered.

And then I fell silent, lost
my voice and couldn't sing
for days. I was useful to no one,

but she came back. Every day
I heard humming as she unlatched
the door, her voice breaking

clean like waves through the room.
Mmm, mmm, mmm, she sang,
checking my temperature,

furiously shaking the mercury
to the bottom, and, Sister,
she whispered, when she thought

I was beyond hearing,
when you going to get up
and give a rat's ass.

OUR COMMON FRIEND

Although it was years ago and she
was a friend of a friend, I recall
her name was Pam. I've forgotten

our common friend's name,
but recall so well the story
she told of a hot tub party

where Pam (this was in the seventies)
was pursued in the public water—
lights turned low and guitars blaring

on the stereo. And under the warm
swirling wet, Pam entertained
the interests of a bass player

from a local metal band whose habit,
we all observed, was to lure women
in the crowd to him by stroking

his greased black moustache (this
was in the seventies) and swaying
his tight-crotch hips, and angling,

just so, a reflective mirror pick-guard
he'd installed on his Fender
precision bass so the spotlight

threw a sharp beam—arcing a triangle
of light from the spot cam
to the pick-guard and into the eyes

of the chosen woman, now blinded
and unable to flee (just as certain
animals stun their prey). That night

Pam drew his attention in the hot tub,
by training her arsenal on him.
(We all admired her iron points,

round and pruned brown,
next to our tawny circles.)
Which gave rise to a moment later

in the cabana—small triangles
of jungle print stripped away,
the ceramic tile, cold and grainy

beneath them. And in the grit
and the growl, he begged her
(she told us later), pleaded for her

to take him home, to soft lights,
to cotton sheets. We all admired
how she silenced his whimpers—

Not here, not like this—forcing him
to bring the jewels into the harsh
public light. Here was our champion,

a woman with breasts like battalions
and a locker room tongue. She,
who is married now, I'm certain,

with a house on a tree-lined street,
kids in college, a self-cleaning oven,
disconnected from this story

as I am from our common friend,
forgotten as we've all become so early
in this next century, even from ourselves.

DYLAN'S LOST YEARS

Somewhere between Hibbing
and New York, the red rust streets
of the iron range and the shipping yards
of the Atlantic, somewhere between
Zimmerman and Dylan was a pit stop
in Fargo, a superman-in-the-phone-booth
interlude, recalled by no one but
the Danforth Brothers who hired
the young musician, fresh in town
with his beat-up six string and his
small-town twang, to play shake,
rattle, and roll, to play good golly,
along with Wayne on keys and Dirk
on bass, two musical brothers
whom you might still find playing
the baby grand, happy hours
at the Southside Holiday Inn.
And if you slip the snifter a five,
Wayne might talk, between how high
the moon, and embraceable you, about
Dylan's lost years, about the Elvis sneer,
the James Dean leather collar pulled
tight around his neck, about the late night
motorcycle rides, kicking over the city's
garbage cans. And how they finally
had to let him go, seeing how he was
more trouble than he was worth,
and with everyone in full agreement
that the new boy just could not sing.

Mooch

When Mooch shows up
at your door, he's carrying that midnight blue,

hard-backed suitcase that his mother got
when she went away to college, the kind

Doris Day pulled out of the closet and never
got fully packed when she became emotional

and decided to run away from Rock Hudson.
In the movie, Rock rushes in and fixes things.

In your real life, Mooch steps in and never
leaves. He lives out of that suitcase. Everything

but his guitars fit between its clever latches—
two pairs of pants, four shirts, and five unmatched

pairs of socks. No underwear, because he doesn't
wear them, and no toothbrush, thank you,

he will just use yours. Isn't it handy how
the case fits under your bed, leaving no trace

of him, except for the constant hand on the remote,
the skinny bottom planted on your couch,

and, oh, how he prides himself for only eating
leftovers out of your crowded refrigerator.

Joe Kohler Wanted to Be

a drummer. His mother kept
a dusty museum of his progress—
the sticks and snare drum heads

that crumbled in his hands,
the self-destructing trap sets.
He liked to eat crunchy foods

close to your ear and read
the newspaper over your back,
whispering disaster into your ears.

He'd settle back on the old green couch
and inhale pot like regular tobacco,
yawning and blowing smoke rings.

He wore paisley shirts and those
brown suede shoes you can buy
on sale at Payless any time of the year.

On the road he learned the art
of whoring around, eventually
overcoming the compulsion

to marry every woman he slept with.
What could we do, he owned half
the P.A. and the yellow van we drove

to gigs in. The day we fired him
it was only because, no matter
how much Joe Kohler wanted to be

a drummer—with his tweed hat,
and his knotted red neckerchief—
he remained absolutely devoid

of any ability to keep a beat, which,
above all other possible charms,
every good drummer must have.

Big Guitar Sound

Although everyone told Randy
he'd have to go to Spain
to get the truly big guitar sound,

the kind that comes barreling
out of the guitar like the bulls
out of the gates at Pamplona,

he thought he'd try Des Moines first,
a place called Last Chance Guitars,
famous for having refused Dylan

use of the bathroom one time back
in the eighties during his Jesus-phase
when he really had to go, but the clerk

didn't recognize the pout behind
the sunglasses that curved, dark
and mirrored, around his famous face.

Everything about Randy was oversized—
massive ham-bone hands, long strike-a-pose
legs, big hair threatening to topple him

as he bent to play a lick, his tongue out,
dreaming of pouring a sound as thick
as cream off his neck. At the Last Chance

he found the metal zone, a row of pedals
all strung together, LEDs popping on
and off like Christmas lights, the flanger

that doubled his tone, made him two
instead of one, still sounding less
than a trip to Spain—the good

that breathing in the air would do.
He tried the baby tremolo, pulsating
through the neck of his guitar. He shook

the life from it, stomping on the chorus,
a thick, shimmering sound rising,
the wah, wah, the super fuzz,

the hyperturbo overdrive grunge
phase shifter that made him sound
like thirteen chain saws gnawing

through walls, a continent away
from Memphis and still not as big
as if he'd gone to Spain.

Do Drop Inn

When they found Keith
in a motel room in Jacksonville,
someone said they had to break
the chain, throw a shoulder against

the dark splinter of wood, force
the metal rings to give up
the mounted gold clasp.
Someone else said the links

were swinging free and the police
walked into an already open
door. Doesn't matter except
to know he wasn't alone

in the end. Jacksonville's hot
this time of year. Keith would've
hated going in a mom-and-pop
Do Drop Inn with a marquee

flashing, *eat, sleep, bowl.*
Those hands could play
the three-over-four, the slide,
the strut, the syncopation,

like nobody could teach. He
was always going to California,
but first the dirty dance halls,
then the pregnant wife.

After that the fat paychecks
on the cocktail circuit
held him, always in debt,
but on the way out and going

to California shortly thereafter.
When I met him, I had a habit
of quitting smoking for twenty
minutes, and he would vow

to leave his wife. In that room
where they found him,
I imagine a woman slipping
out from under and collecting

her clothes. She slides
the chain free and runs down
the hallway, falling apart
as she runs, falling apart as she runs

away from Keith and the way
he knew how to play.

THE DAY MONTANA TURNED

The day Montana turned into a movie was bleak,
    overcast, a silent, windless day of people moving
        through intersections all morning, crossing over

but never once colliding. I wore sunglasses
    behind charcoal-tinted windows in the black van,
        angle parked on Third Street as he took his wounded

keyboard into the repair shop. So, maybe I did empty
    a Tequila Sunrise into its guts the night before,
        and maybe not-so-accidentally. He and everything

in my sight belonged to his wife, or so she informed me
    over her crystal phone, comfortable back home
        with her Audi and her fox terriers. And when the cool

juice hit the hot wires, maybe I did enjoy the slight
    crackling sound, the burnt wire smell, and the tiny
        blue plume that rose from the circuits like a minor

explosion. Everything's expensive, I hissed in his ear
    as he bent to eye the catastrophe. And maybe
        that's why he slugged me extra hard that night

as I sat in the bathtub, my body slippery from soap,
    scrubbing the layers of salt that settled like fine grain
        under my skin. So the next morning we went

downtown to see what could be done for the keyboard,
    and I sat in the truck wearing sunglasses to cover the explosion
        of orange to red to maroon that was blossoming

on my face. On the street, people moved through
        intersections like sleepwalkers, never once colliding.
            Their faces, covered with mufflers, chuffed cold smoke

into the air like clouds in need of dialogue. I tried to read their breath,
        but there were no words. It was not cartoon, it was movie,
            reeling silently by as I sat in the van unable to step out,

afraid to be lost without even this nothing left to me.

Turning to Herself

She doubts the succession
of circles, the deep grooves,
like stories within stories

that the garbled reflection
of the rest area mirror tells.
The lines rim her eyes adding up

to zero, for she cannot recall
when this roadmap gathered
on her face. The sleep of years

upon her, she trips from
the van into this late night
rest stop, hungry for candy

and relief, stalled out on
the porcelain tiles, the flush
and flushing from the cold

row of stalls. The dim light
tells a story of smooth, unbroken
flight, gliding unobstructed

along surfaces, all leading
to this catalogue of travel,
this book whose spine

she's never cracked. The circles
show movement, like rings
inside the trunk, revealing

what the surface conceals—
the dry years, the crisscrosses,
the circle backs, the pockmarks—

all signs of terrain traveled
but not recalled. Turning to
herself she puts her hands

to her face, as if touching
Braille, turning to herself
she reads her own story

for the first time.

THIS NEW QUIET

The day after the fire, all their equipment
charred in a ditch and blown to ashes,
the thin axle of the truck lying on its side

like the burnt-out frame of a dragonfly,
they gathered in a circle of old couches,
most of them sitting forward, their eyes

studying the swirls in the worn carpet.
They who had the power to make
so much noise sat in this new quiet.

In voices ringing flat as the many roads
they'd traveled, they tried out the new
words the fire left on their tongues.

They did not speak of debt or creditors,
nor did they speak of lost guitars—the blond
Les Paul, and the rosewood Gibson double-neck

that sang sweetly in its velvet case
as it rolled down the highway. They sat
in silence. Outside traffic rushed by,

the drone and clatter of passing trains,
the honk of angry horns as the sun dialed
around the room, angling a view through

the windows. Finally, someone stood.
It was the tall blond guitar player
who rose, wobbly in his black boots.

He stood in the center of the spiral,
raised his thin hands to his face and
blew out one long exhale. It hissed

through the room like a wild balloon
losing steam. When all the wind was
out of him, he gulped one deep breath,

swung a long arm like a knockout punch
through the sheer emptiness of air,
and said, *Fuck*. It was only

one word. It was inadequate
for the moment. But it was
a good place to start.

THE WAY OF FIRE

Every year you give your mother
candles for Christmas. You buy her
brass nightlamps, pewter votives,

marble hurricane lamps. Every year
you watch her pick through the package,
lift the thing into the air. Lovely,

she says and finds a place on one of her
cool, clean surfaces. How to explain
this distance you have come

so far from the tow of her waters.
How to introduce this other mother
who has licked you clean with

her violent tongue? Every year
you return to unlit wicks, still white,
pressed neatly into the smooth tips

of tapers. Even on these holidays
of eggnog and sitting in circles,
all your gifts unused. She's worried

about wax drippings and burn holes
and whether or not the drapery
will catch. Besides, what good is fire,

she asks, when we have light already?

Palimpsest

You are here.
——Notation on Concourse Maps

Let Y be your destination, the unnamed
place beyond the flickering fluorescence
of corridors, the terrazzo floors worn smooth

from the shoes of the dead. Let X be
your present location, the uncharted
space between pencil and chalk marks,

the keypad's incessant clatter. Listen,
you are here, a blip on a screen, transfixed
between home and away. It is possible

to create a life, doors opening to other
doors, the fresh breeze of tomorrow
rushing in to make the world new

each day. The canvas remembers
its maker, inside the hairline grooves
under the brushstrokes live the barest

traces—whispered thoughts, words
spoken, mundane as groceries, bills
and gasoline. The fingerprints

of the dead are everywhere, the tiny
whorls like plots to cities where one
could spend a life. Best to find

your own path, chart the roadmap
etched under your skin, sit down,
get to know the wantings of your feet.

On the Corner
of Hunger and Thirst

I've read about the all-consuming ferocious love
of the original parents who gazed upon their young

with such relish and delight that all they could think
to do was eat them. And this is when, the story goes,

God took down his work papers, touched his pencil
to his tongue, and reduced by forty percent the intensity

of parental love. Still I've felt this way about kittens,
that awful crush of love, wanting to squeeze them

to death in their cuteness. And I've seen husbands
wriggle from the grip of love's terrible claw. Oh, rare friend,

brother, I was after something exquisite that would break
with taste on my tongue those afternoons we talked,

the light outside turning from blue to sapphire to deep
indigo, my lips pressed close to your ear whispering

our words into stillness. I was after that mix of salt
and blood between us, something more than this dry

paper life, the feel of gristle on our tongues,
like the swish of whiskey and sirloin late at night

after everyone who doesn't know how to party
has left the party. Once I ate a cheeseburger

with raw onions and mayonnaise so sublime,
I have searched for it since that night, tripping

on chocolate mesc when Dave Eggen found me
jammed into a phone booth on Highway 3,

a halo of hungry moths circling the ghostly globe.
I was pumping dimes into the slot, trying to win

that big, communications lotto, my fingers hallucinating
their way into sleeping bedrooms, darkened kitchens

where wives in curlers, husbands in torn underwear
rose to hear me rave about the absolute transforming

power of the latest southern shipment. That's when
Dave Eggen folded me into his Fury and drove to

the café where he knew enough to order me the #6
that sizzled wise and inscrutable in its bed of fries,

just as you arrived, your voice coming over the line
in twists and turns, digressions and variations.

Oh sweet five by five, we extemporized there
where we met on the corner of hunger and thirst.

Me, with my flask of buried teas, and you with your
sweet bits of jerky. Remember, back in the day

when we were all ears, eyes, and hands for each other.

Acknowledgments

Grateful acknowledgments to the editors of the magazines in which the following poems first appeared, sometimes in earlier versions:

Connecticut Review:	"Drats"
Cumberland Poetry Review:	"This New Quiet" (under the title, "Airband"), "Envy of Origins," "Light Sweet Crude," "My Catholic Tongue," "Hurricane," and "Alchemy"
Half Tones to Jubilee:	"Big Guitar Sound"
Kalliope:	"Other Knowledge"
Many Mountains Moving:	"On the Corner of Hunger and Thirst" and "Usual Magic"
Mississippi Review:	"Do Drop Inn" and "Beating Up the Brother"
North American Review:	"Within Moments"
Passages North:	"More Like Hunger"
Red Weather:	"The Hardness of Math" and "From Sweetness"
River City:	"The Falling Man"
South Dakota Review:	"My Husband, a City Boy, Decides to Buy a Truck"
Southern Poetry Review:	"Turning to Herself"
Spoon River Anthology:	"Dylan's Lost Years"
Threepenny Review:	"On Lake Superior"
Witness:	"Wearing Dead Women's Clothes" and "The Day Montana Turned"

"Older Sister" and "How Bad News Comes" appeared in *The Talking of Hands: New Rivers 30th Anniversary Anthology*. Minneapolis: New Rivers Press, 1998.

"Big Guitar Sound," "Dylan's Lost Years," "Do Drop Inn," and "This New Quiet" first appeared, in slightly different versions, in *The Hunger Bone: Rock & Roll Stories*. Minneapolis: New Rivers Press, 2001.

"Palimpsest" was commissioned by the Iowa State University Museums, to accompany a public art project, Doug Shelton's mural, *Unlimited Possibilities*, 1997.

The author wishes to thank the Ragdale Foundation, the Ucross Foundation, the Iowa Arts Council, and Iowa State University for grants and fellowships which enabled this work to be completed.

Special thanks to Pearl Editions, especially Marilyn Johnson and Dorianne Laux for their early support of the manuscript. Thanks also to the following poets whose work inspires and whose friendship sustains me: Philip Bryant, Barbara Crow, Glenna Henderson, and Sheryl St. Germain.

DEBRA MARQUART, an associate professor of English at Iowa State University, is the poetry editor of *Flyway Literary Review*. Marquart's two previous books are *Everything's a Verb: Poems* (New Rivers Press, 1995), and *The Hunger Bone: Rock & Roll Stories* (New Rivers Press, 2001). Since the 1970s, Marquart has performed and toured with rock and heavy metal bands. She's currently a collaborating member of a jazz-poetry, rhythm & blues project, The Bone People, with whom she released two CDs in 1996: *Orange Parade* (acoustic/ alternative rock), and *A Regular Dervish* (spoken word/ jazz poetry).